MW01710769

Dear Paula,

I hope this book helps you Function, Feel and Live Better!

Dr Pete

FUNCTION BETTER, FEEL BETTER, LIVE BETTER.

How you can maximize the health and longevity of your body, spine and joints with chiropractic.

by

Peter Angerilli, B.Sc., D.C.

www.clearviewchiropractic.ca
https://www.youtube.com/drpeterangerilli

The information in this book is for educational purposes only. The information in this book is based on my own personal experiences practicing as a Doctor of Chiropractic and interpretations of available research. The information in this book should not be taken as medical or health care advice or solicitation for chiropractic services.
If you have any health issues or concerns please consult with a chiropractor or your physician. Always consult your chiropractor or physician before beginning or making any changes in your lifestyle and consult your medical physician for advice regarding medications.
Please also note the author has great respect for all healthcare practitioners and acknowledges that relief from pain and suffering and improved performance can be achieved from a variety of methods including chiropractic, physiotherapy, other manual therapists, exercise, medication, psychology, yoga, meditation and more. His assertion is that chiropractic care is not the only way to achieve improvements in function and feeling but chiropractic spinal and joint adjusting are a unique way that may not be widely recognized or understood by the public.

Contents

Introduction

"A man is born gentle and weak; at his death he is hard and stiff. All things, including the grass and trees, are soft and pliable in life: dry and brittle in death. Stiffness is thus a companion of death; flexibility a companion of life...a tree that cannot bend with crack in the wind."
Lao-Tzu

Hi I'm Dr. Pete Angerilli. I'm a 46 year old male who wakes pretty much every day feeling great. No back pain. No joint stiffness. No headaches. No neck and shoulder tension. Most days I also go to bed feeling this way - feeling great! I also don't need to take any prescription or over the counter medications. I can't say this for most of my contemporaries. And I wasn't always this way. In fact, I had my first migraine headache at 7 years old. I had my first back spasm when I was in the 9th grade. I was at my friend's house and when I went to get up off the couch my back completely seized. Kind of embarrassing for a 14 year old! By age 19 from playing football and heavy weight lifting I had developed right shoulder tendonitis along with daily neck pain and stiffness. I probably took more Advil and Tylenol in my first 20 years than most people should take in their entire life!

I didn't exactly get off to the healthiest start during my first 20 years on planet earth. But I had a very fortunate thing happen to me in my last month of high school. We had a guest speaker in Phys Ed class who introduced me to an entirely different way of looking at health. You see to that point health care for me had consisted of visits to the family doctor or emergency room which always ended in a drug prescription. Although some of the medications had helped with my symptoms, none had provided a long term solution for me. As you probably know, drugs that control symptoms like pain and inflammation can't really get to the source of the problems in our body and solve them.

I'm sure you are wondering - just who was this guest speaker whose message changed my life? It was ...a Chiropractor! I ended up becoming a patient of the chiropractor, a wonderful man named Dr. Bruce Walton and over time found a solution to my 20 plus years of aches, pains and injuries.

I was so impressed with what chiropractic care, specifically chiropractic adjustments had done for my well-being that I decided to become a chiropractor. I did have a few detours on the way though, things that I think have actually given me an edge to become a compassionate and skilled Doctor...

In my University days I got a job as an autopsy assistant which was an invaluable opportunity to study anatomy close up on "fresh" specimens. I also worked as a research assistant in a neurophysiology lab at the University of Guelph where I learned a lot about how the nervous system factors into normal body function.

I also worked as a Police Officer for two years. Yes, I told you I got sidetracked! I went into policing to try and help people but realized that all too often the "criminals" I was dealing with were regular people that got off track many years before they got into trouble. Arresting them was really just applying a short term bandage to a societal problem which rarely resulted in long term improvements. I think you are probably starting to learn that I am not into quick fixes that don't get to the cause of a problem. I also was surprised to learn that a great deal of my police time was spent dealing with those struggling with mental health issues. It didn't take me long to decide that if I was going to help society in the way I wanted to it would have to be working with people on more of a proactive basis - helping to correct and stabilize their physical and mental health before it spiraled out of control.

I went back to school and completed my Doctor of Chiropractic degree in 2005.
I started as a practicing chiropractor and have been helping my patients for over 15 years solve their health problems and prevent future ones. My motto is that when you function better, and feel better, you can be as close as possible to the 100% best version of yourself. This makes life better for you, your family, friends, co-workers and your community.

That's my story. Well, truth be told my story continues to evolve every day I am in the office. You see they call it "practice" for a reason - the amazing thing about my career is that you can continually learn from patient encounters and new science that emerges every day about how to better help people function and feel better. I wrote this book out of sheer appreciation for what chiropractic has done for my life, for my patients' lives and what it can do for our future health and well-being.

So enough about me, it's time to talk about your story. Why are you reading this book? Chances are it's because you've had an ache, pain or problem that you haven't found a long term solution for. Or maybe you are interested in living a long healthy life and safeguarding your ability to function and feel good for as long as possible. Or maybe you're just curious - what could possibly be so interesting about chiropractic that this guy wrote a whole book on it! Whatever the reason, it is my sincere wish that you find something in these pages that will help you function better, feel better and live better!

Chapter 1 - Why the pain may not be the problem

For many of you reading this book I know that if I asked you: "If I could wave a magic wand and give you anything you desire" your answer would be "Get rid of my pain!"

Pain sucks. In all its places and forms. Whether it's a tight low back which causes stabbing pain when you move, or the thigh and leg burning of sciatica, or the throbbing head pain with a headache or migraine...I could go on but you get the picture. The worst part about pain is that it stops you from being you. There's no way you can drive a golf ball, get in a good workout, take care of your children, or get a good night's rest when you are living with pain. Pain affects your home life, as well as your work and social life. If you have a physical job like working in construction, in a factory, retail environment or job where you have to lift, bend, walk and move, pain can be a major issue. Similarly, if your job requires you to sit for long periods in front of a computer, pain and stiffness can become really annoying and distracting to your concentration and productivity.

What have you tried for pain relief?
Let me guess here...painkillers, anti-inflammatories, supplements, stretches, therapies, foam rolling or other "do it yourself" devices...sound familiar? All of these things have their place and may have given you temporarily relief.

Here's what you need to know though: Your pain is not your problem. Yes I said it, ***your pain is not your problem!*** You are probably saying to yourself right now "Dr. Pete, my pain is my problem, what do you know about it anyway?"

Remember though, I lived with back and neck pain, stiffness, migraines and shoulder pain for many years. So I know what you are going through to some extent.

What I am getting at here is that pain is a signal experienced by your brain that something in your body isn't functioning properly. I think you'd have to agree to be a true statement.

So instead of asking "what will take away my pain" we can ask a better question: "how can I find what is causing my pain and deal with the source of it?"

Good question! Now that we are on the same page, we are going to look at causes of pain. It's pretty obvious that if you put your hand on a hot stove or twist your ankle while walking the immediate sensation of pain tells your brain about possible tissue damage and how to prevent any further damage from occurring (i.e. get your hand off the stove or stop walking on a damaged ankle).

From here on out however we're going to be looking at the more chronic pains mentioned above like those experienced by sufferers of neck pain, back pain, headaches, joint pains and sciatica.

But...to understand what can go wrong in our body we FIRST have to understand what a properly functioning body works like. So let's do that now!

Chapter 2 - Health Equals Function

Our bodies are amazing creations. When we are conceived we grow in nine months from a sperm and an egg to a 30 trillion celled, multi system organism that performs countless tasks every minute just to keep us alive. So much of what our body does every day like digesting food, filtering our blood, eliminating toxins, fighting off harmful bacteria and viruses, healing cell damage, pumping blood and even breathing are pretty much done by the one system that controls and coordinates our body. That system is...Our Nerve System!

The human brain, spinal cord and nerves is one of the most fantastic structures we know of in the Universe. Science is really just starting to scratch the surface in understanding how our nerve system and bodies function.

The Chiropractic profession has recognized the importance of the nerve system since its inception over 100 years ago. Many of the early chiropractic writings refer to the importance of brain communication with the cells of the body for proper function and health. Recent research however has indicated that probably the most important factor in health and function, especially of our muscles and joints, requires proper body to brain feedback. Our muscles, ligaments, tendons, joints and organs have innumerable nerve receptors embedded in them that give continuous feedback to the brain 24/7. This feedback is an absolute necessity to allow for proper movement, coordination, strength and function.

The College of Chiropractors in Ontario, where I practice defines the practice of chiropractic as:

“The assessment of conditions related to the spine, nervous system and joints and the diagnosis, prevention and treatment, primarily by adjustment of: dysfunctions or disorders arising from the structures or functions of the spine and the effects of those dysfunctions or disorders on the nervous system; and dysfunctions or disorders arising from the structures or functions of the joints [1].”

When the joints of our spine and extremities are functioning normally, your brain can receive all of the important information needed to control and coordinate your body. When one or more of your joints begins to lose their normal function, there can be loss of body to brain communication, leading to errors in brain output. This can ultimately lead to things like abnormal muscle tension, weakness, injury, cell damage and…PAIN!

The thing that most people fail to realize (because they are never taught this concept) is that changes in joint and nerve system function usually occur slowly and without people noticing it. So we have a situation where your body is slowly losing its normal function and you aren’t aware that it’s happening until you start feeling pain or get injured doing something simple like bending over the sink to brush your teeth or picking up a piece of paper.

So…I hope you now realize that your pain and symptoms usually come after your body, specifically your joints, muscles and nerves have not been functioning properly for a while. Like was the case with me, you don’t have to be “old” for this to happen. Abnormal joint function can happen early in life or develop later in life.

This brings us to the next question: what causes our joints to stop functioning normally?

Chapter 3 - The Stresses of Life

Back when I first opened my practice I used to speak at local workplaces teaching people about how everyday activities might be affecting their spine and nerve system. My talk was titled "Stress and Your Life" and I really enjoyed getting the message to people that health problems were usually caused by their lifestyle which could be modified to improve their wellbeing.

Let's define "stress" as some force outside the body that is either intense enough OR repeated often enough to cause damage to the body altering it's function. Stress impacts our body when these external forces exceed the tolerance of the tissues of the body, thereby giving way to cell damage and tissue injury.

Stress for me started at hour zero when I was pulled out of my mother and into this world by forceps. The stress of the forceps yanking on my neck damaged my neck muscles and joints so I never really even started 100% healthy. The loss of ability of my neck joints to function normally and subsequent nerve irritation set me up for the migraine headaches I would later develop at 7 years of age.

There aren't many forceps births that happen anymore BUT one stress that is unique for kids today is the ever increasing physical demands that competitive sports place on their developing joints. My three kids have experienced thousands of hours and millions of repetitions of kicking soccer balls, swinging baseball bats and performing tumbling routines in cheerleading that undoubtedly stressed their joints and bodies way more than the kids of 20 or

30 years ago. If your kids are like mine and play recreational and competitive sports, you might be wondering how to know if your kids' joints are functioning normally? The answer is simple. Bring them to a chiropractor who can do a detailed assessment and look for problems before they cause issues later in life. Oh, and if you want to give your kids an edge in sports and life, spinal and joints exams and adjustments when needed will not only help them prevent future problems but will also help them perform their best now. This again relates to making sure their joints are fully functioning thereby maximizing the brain to body coordination that is needed for skill development in physical activities.

If you are thinking "my kids have been to the family doctor for checkups, they seem fine" then that's great. But I have to ask, was your child actually physically examined? Was their posture checked? Joint ranges of motion? Was a hands on examination done to see how their spine and soft tissues are working? If not, then you really don't know. An actual physical exam is needed to make conclusions about the health and function of joints, muscles and nerves. This information can't be ascertained by asking a few questions and certainly can't be reached through phone or virtual consults that are becoming popular today.

Now back to you - so maybe you weren't a forceps birth and didn't do much in the way of childhood physical activity. Well, there are the everyday stresses you've been dealing with in adulthood that may have compromised your joint and nerve system function.

We can divide these stresses into two main categories: Microtraumas and Macrotraumas.

Macrotraumas like the name implies involve major force impacts to tissues which usually cause immediate cell damage and injury. This would be things like car accidents, trauma from sports (i.e. getting body checked), falls, and things like strain/sprain from heavy lifting as is seen in activities like powerlifting and crossfit.

Microtraumas to joints and soft tissues include things like repetitive strains, postural strains and prolonged immobility. The classic example here is the person that sits at a desk all day and repetitively uses a mouse to do their job. Let's also not forget the more recent problem of forward head posture seen with smart phone use - so called "text neck". Loss of joint movement is particularly problematic because the cells of our soft tissues adapt based on the forces that go through them. The idea here is that if we don't regularly move our joints through their full ranges of motion, they become limited as the tissues become shortened, calcified or fibrotic (scar tissue). The old adage "use it or lose it" applies here.

So as we don't move our joints fully, they lose their mobility, become stiff AND consequently we get loss of signals from nerve receptors in the joints and surrounding tissues. Your joints also need to move daily to maintain their health, as movement pumps in fluid which provides them with nutrition and lubrication [2]. Chronic lack of joint movement alters normal joint function leading to stiffness, susceptibility to injury and eventually PAIN. If your joints don't move through their normal full ranges of motion for a really long time (like years) or become chronically stressed and misaligned we can get degenerative changes - the dreaded osteoarthritis [3]. Not what you want if you want to function and feel well!

We can of course also develop abnormal joint mechanics from repetitive strains from things like running, cycling, gardening and housekeeping. In these cases we may get inflammation to joints which often causes reflex muscle tightening around the joint leading to tightness and swelling.

You might also be wondering...What is the role of psychological stress in joint problems?

Here's a hypothetical example to help you understand this question. Imagine I have two patients, Sarah and Sally. Sarah gets chronic headaches and neck pain, on average 2-3 times per week, and has for close to ten years. Sally similarly gets chronic headaches on average 2-3 times per week, and has for close to ten years. So with respect to health problems Sarah and Sally are similar. I examine Sarah and Sally and find both to have forward head posture, as well as irritation and dysfunction of the joints in the upper neck - a common finding in people with headaches that when corrected with chiropractic adjustments often lessens headache frequency and intensity and sometimes completely gets rid of them. Here's a key difference though in how Sarah and Sally will respond to my care. Sarah is relatively happy, enjoys her work and kids and is generally not too stressed most of the time. Sally however has a very demanding job, tension in her relationship, difficulties with her family and a history of psychological traumas from her past along with a habit of worrying about her health frequently. Which of these two women will likely respond better to their chiropractic care with respect to headache relief? I can tell you from my clinical experience that Sally will almost undoubtedly be the more challenging patient to help get relief. This doesn't mean that she can't be helped. In fact, many of my patients who've been the happiest with their care are those that have to deal with significant ongoing stress. For them, chiropractic care and the lifestyle recommendations I've given them often keep them able to continue functioning at home and work. This is called supportive care - care that if not provided would cause a person's condition to deteriorate to unsatisfactory levels.

It didn't take me too long in practice to realize that one of my biggest jobs as a chiropractor is to be an ear for my patients. Chiropractors have a unique role in their patients' lives as we usually see them fairly often over months or years, much more than the average person sees for their medical doctor or dentist. In a sense we become part of their family, sharing in their high points and low points of life. I appreciate and take very seriously my role in this capacity and always work to help coach my patients when I can and help them manage their life stresses. It's really satisfying to see my patients make incremental changes not only in their physical health but also in the areas of mental and emotional health as we work together over time. As my patients are able to function better in the various physical and emotional areas of their lives, they get to experience more well-being day to day. They are excited about life and it feels good to get up in the morning!

To better understand stress and how it affects our health I have to teach you a little bit about your nerve system. Your nerve system has two divisions: sympathetic and parasympathetic. For simplicity's sake we can describe the sympathetic nerve system as being active during "fight or flight" situations. Your parasympathetic nerve system is active when you are resting/digesting/healing. Some scientists believe that humans should spend most of the time in parasympathetic mode except when we are exercising or dealing with acute stressful situations. Some also hypothesize that nerve system imbalance (i.e. being in a state of stress/sympathetic activation chronically) may be underlying many major diseases including heart disease, diabetes and auto-immune disorders [4]. A book written a few years ago entitled “Why Zebras don’t get Ulcers” explains in detail how humans, unlike animals, can experience chronic mental stress that is linked to many diseases [5].

Another thing that sympathetic nerve system activation does is increase muscle tension in our neck, back, arms and legs to prepare us to “fight or flee”. That’s a really great thing to have happen when we need to sprint across a road to avoid getting hit by a car, but you can imagine that if your muscles are chronically tense due to work stress, relationship stress, financial stress, family stress (I could go on) then the tension this will put on your joints will limit their motion leading to the problems mentioned above like back pain, neck pain and headaches.

Obviously you can’t go back in time and undo all of the stresses that your body has experienced in your lifetime. What you can do however is with the help of a chiropractor RESTORE your joint and related nerve system function to as close to normal as possible. In restoring normal function to your body, very often your symptoms will subside. This means less to no pain, as well as a good feeling body that is up to any day to day tasks that you have to or want to do.

My favorite thing as a chiropractor is knowing that I can help people get back to the life they love by improving their joint and nerve system function!

Chapter 4 - What gets you out of bed in the morning?

Like I said in the last chapter my reason to get out of bed in the morning and into my office is the feeling I get from knowing that I can help people like you function and feel better.

This takes many shapes and forms depending on the individual. But here are a few of my favorite examples:

- helping a mom get clear of headaches so she can be the loving caregiver she desperately wants to be to her kids
- Helping the gym rat overcome the chronic spine strains so they can train consistently to be strong fit, and looking great
- Helping the grandparent improve their back and hip stiffness so they can get on the floor and play with their grandkids
- Helping the nurse get well from sciatica so she can get through a 12+ hour shift on her feet caring for her patients
- Helping the man who lives for golf get rid of his back pain so he can enjoy every hole!

These are just a few examples of the ways that restoring healthy joint and nerve function might make life better for you. Why? So you can do the thing that gets you out of bed in the morning!

Our passions, be they caring for our kids, being great in our career or enjoying leisure activities are what bring us joy in life.

It's a real shame when pain and stiffness prevent us from living the life we love. But, I hope you are beginning to see that chiropractic care could be the answer to steering you clear of these problems and keeping you that way.

Chapter 5 - Would you drive 3 hours for a chiropractic adjustment?

If you're old enough you might remember a TV commercial from the 1980's for Hair Club for Men where the owner says "I'm not only the president of Hair Club for Men, I'm also a client!" When it comes to chiropractic - that's me, I not only love to adjust my patients, I also love getting adjusted! In fact when I was in chiropractic school I had a favorite chiropractor that I'd make the three plus hour drive from Toronto to Kingston just to have his magic hands do their work on me!

With chiropractic care being a very hands on interaction I know that like happened to me, people get attached to their Doctor and will drive a long time to see one they connect with. I have a number of patients who drive over an hour to see me - not necessarily because I am so good but probably because they feel comfortable with me and have established a trust in me and my office. There are plenty of great Doctors of Chiropractic in every city but I certainly get it when people don't mind travelling long distances to see one of their choosing.

There's nothing quite like the feeling you get after a good chiropractic adjustment. I can only describe it as an overwhelming feeling of ease of mind and body. It's led some people to speculate that "chiropractic adjustments might be addictive" because they feel so good that it keeps people coming back for more. As I write this in 2020, one of the biggest growing areas of YouTube are videos of spine and joint adjustments being done to patients. It seems even watching other people get adjusted can bring us feelings of satisfaction and wellbeing!

I should of course mention that not everyone who receives a chiropractic adjustment loves the feeling. There are a number of possible reasons for this. One has to do with the state of your spine when you get adjusted. If your joints are stiff, arthritic and inflamed, or if you have a lot of nerve system and muscle tension, an adjustment can be an intense, uncomfortable, even jarring experience. A good chiropractor takes this into account and uses methods that are appropriate for the individual at a particular time in their care. If I have a new patient with the above mentioned problems I know we are going to have to work very gently for a while to get some mobility into their spinal joints in a way that will cause minimal discomfort.

Not everybody of course loves the “crack”. Some of my patients have told me they can’t stand the sound and feeling of their joints popping as occurs during many adjusting procedures. This is completely fine, and for those patients we use either drop table or instrument adjusting which causes no “crack” but still activates the nerve system and improves joint function.

By the way, the “crack” is better described as an audible release or “cavitation” which research tells us represents the quick separation of joint surfaces that occurs when the chiropractor introduces a force into a spinal joint. Many of my patients really like the feeling of this happening during their adjustment and report an immediate change in terms of lessening pain and stiffness as well as bring a feeling of satisfaction and wellbeing as previously mentioned.

Chiropractors aren’t limited to adjusting joints, they may also use other methods including soft tissue therapies, stretching, exercises, acupuncture or electrical modalities.

Bottom line is your chiropractor can find methods that can help you function and feel better in a way that is safe and comfortable for you!

Chapter 6 - A Brief History of Hands on Healing and Chiropractic

Humans have used hands on techniques for thousands of years to alleviate suffering and help with healing. Direct evidence of manipulation of spines and joints dates back to ancient Greece (400 BC) where the writings of Hippocrates describe techniques to help with spinal problems [6]. In my practice I have had patients from India, Trinidad and Jamaica tell me of “bonesetters” from their villages who would adjust their spines and joints for everything from sprains to stomach aches. They always say it the same way: “Dr. Pete, what they did looks really similar to your adjustments!” How lucky for them they didn’t need 8 years of post-secondary schooling and $100,000+ in student loans to be certified to practice!

In the 1800’s two professions were born that recognized the relationships between the structure of the spine and joints and the health of the body: namely Chiropractic and Osteopathy. By the way, patients sometimes ask me what the difference is between seeing an osteopath or a chiropractor today. Although both practitioners have the intent to improve body function with hands on methods, I can’t really comment on the specific differences without knowing what an individual provider is actually doing to patients in their office. I can say however that in Ontario, Chiropractic is a regulated health profession, with standards on training, licensing and scope of practice developed by the College of Chiropractors of Ontario and the Ministry of Health. Currently there in Ontario the practice of Osteopathy is not a government regulated health profession.

Getting back to the 1800's...In 1895 a Canadian name D.D. Palmer, who was working as a healer in Davenport, Iowa was wrapping up his day when he started chatting with the janitor in his office. The janitor, named Harvey Lillard mentioned that while bending over to clean 17 years prior he strained his back and felt a "pop" after which he became deaf. Palmer wondered about the connection between the "pop" in Lillard's back and the hearing loss. He examined Lillard, found what he thought was a vertebrae out of alignment and pushed on in for three consecutive days. Miraculously, Lillard's healing returned! [7] The first successful adjustment was delivered and chiropractic was born!

D.D. Palmer initially believed he had discovered a cure for deafness and started to solicit patients with hearing loss. If you're wondering how on earth moving a bone in the spine could affect hearing, modern science helps us understand that the change could have happened due to normalization of nerve circuits in the brainstem and spinal cord that follow a spinal manual input [8].

Palmer soon found out that he didn't have a cure for hearing loss, but did discover that pushing on "lumps and bumps" in the spine seemed to bring help to patients with a large variety of health problems [7]. D.D. made sure he had access to books on anatomy and physiology of the time and began to reason that his adjustments must be helping his patients by removing interference to the spinal cord and nerves that ran through and around the spinal bones [7]. So from its earliest days chiropractic hasn't so much been about bones and joints but nerves!

Under the guidance of D.D. Palmer and his son B.J. Palmer, thousands of chiropractors were trained across the United States and Canada. The profession grew rapidly and in the early 1900's brought relief to many individuals who were suffering and couldn't find help through traditional medical means at the time.

B.J. Palmer had a very scientific orientation and from the 1930's to 1950's ran a chiropractic in-patient research clinic. B.J. hired medical doctors and nurses to examine new patients and diagnose them, after which they had a chiropractic evaluation to attempt to determine the spinal problems related to their disease. Palmer pioneered the use of spinal x-ray and used it to determine the specific location of "vertebral subluxations" that were thought to be causing pain and loss of health. It may sound crazy today but there are records of nearly every disease imaginable responding positively to spinal adjustments [9]. B.J. Palmer used advanced medical tests for the time including blood work and ECG (electrocardiogram) to prove to the medical establishment that chiropractic was indeed capable of changing a patient's physiology, with the results not just being "in the patient's head" (placebo effect). B.J's research methods were advanced for the 1940's but of course don't completely stand up to more modern ways such as we see with today's clinical trials. But I do find it interesting that in 400 BC, 1940 or 2020 we can get amazing changes in health and wellbeing when we move a person's spine with an adjustment!

There were also a number of chiropractic hospitals that operated across the U.S. from the 1920's to 60's. One of them was called "Clear View Sanitarium". Clear View was a chiropractic hospital that took in patients who were suffering from "nervous and mental disorders" as they were called at that time. Patients received chiropractic adjustments to try and help calm their nerve system and could also do things like go for walks outside and participate in work duties as their condition improved [10]. In the field of mental health these were very caring and compassionate measures at a time when traditional medicine had little to offer except putting patients in unsanitary asylums where they were often subject to abuse and neglect [10]. I was so impressed when I heard about Clear View back in Chiropractic school that I decided to name my practice "Clearview". Why? Because in some ways I feel like the care we provide is "ahead of our time".

Eventually due to changes in medical insurance and lack of funding all of the chiropractic in-patient institutions closed down [10, 11]. Patients often ask me, "Dr. Pete, how come there aren't chiropractors on staff in hospitals? Not to treat disease but to provide care for spinal and joint problems for individuals who are stuck in an in-patient setting?" It is a good question, and I don't have a good answer. I sure hope it happens in the future.

Thanks for sticking with me on this historical review of hands on healing and the chiropractic profession. Now we're going to fast forward to today...

Chapter 7 - New research uncovers how old methods got results!

For many years chiropractors believed that the results seen after an adjustment were due to the "release of nerve pressure" when a bone was moved off a nerve. We know today although this is possible it is not the mechanism that usually happens during a chiropractic adjustment.

So what is it that actually happens when a chiropractor applies a manual force input into the body of a patient?

There are two things that we can say with confidence that we know are going on. The first one of these is, ***mechanotransduction***.

Okay, mechanotransduction is a big word. What the heck does it mean and why might it be important to you?

"Mechanotransduction focuses on the mechanism by which physical and chemical signals interplay to control how individual cells alter their growth, differentiation, function, or death [12]." The study of mechanotransduction is a relatively new field of inquiry [13] but has been gaining attention in the scientific community over the past 20 years.

From a physical standpoint we can say that forces experienced by the cells in your body can be generated internally (voluntary movement/exercise) or they can be externally applied (i.e. chiropractic adjustment or other hands on therapies).

A word on cells. Do you know you are made of cells? Do you know what a cell is? Think back to grade 9 biology...can't remember? No problem, I'll give you a refresher!

Take a look at this picture of my family taken 4 years ago:

I can tell you that today, we are all LITERALLY different people than we were in this picture.

What I mean is that a large number, if not the majority of the cells in our bodies four years ago have been replaced. Bet you didn't know that! When old cells are replaced by new ones, there is opportunity for changes in their structural organization and function. If the mechanical and chemical forces experienced by our cells stays the same, the pattern for new cells and thus the structure of our muscles, tendons, ligaments etc. remains unchanged. Said another way we are changing, on a cellular level, just to the same thing. So we experience that as being stuck in the same good functioning, or poor functioning body. IF however we change the mechanical inputs to our cells, by regular stretching, exercises, chiropractic adjustments or other manual therapies, often enough, over enough time, our cellular structure and thus tissue function can change. That dear readers is VERY EXCITING NEWS for you and I!

This literally means that chronically tight and stiff soft tissues can over time become more flexible, pliable, elastic, in a sense, younger. And let's go back to the quote from Lao-Tzu in the introduction. The experience of youth goes with flexibility, while aging is experienced by lack of movement and stiffness. Said another way, you are only as young or old as you feel!

We know from animal experiments that limiting motion to the spine results in joint adhesions (scar tissue formation) and osteophytic (bone spur) growth aka arthritis in only 8 weeks [14, 15]. Chiropractors have long asserted that loss of segmental spinal motion will lead to stiffness and degenerative changes in the joints, discs and tissues over time if not corrected. Again, the saying "use it or lose it applies.

There is also some research demonstrating that when we do change the forces experienced by our tissues, those tissues will adapt and change to meet the new demands. This is seen in the phenomenon of "ligamentization", where hamstring tendons used as grafts in anterior cruciate ligament (ACL) knee surgery repair change their cellar structure so that they transform over time into ligament like tissue [16]. Findings like this are so exciting because they point to the possibility that as we change how we use our body we can literally remodel our tissues to be better functioning and feeling.

This also fits with the clinical observations of chiropractors that show that improvements in range of motion and mobility seen when chiropractic adjustments and mobility exercises are applied over time. I want to point out here that time and repetition are the key principles that must be adhered to in order to get a long lasting change in tissue characteristics leading to stable improvements in function and feeling.

Here's a few simple analogies to help you understand this principle:

Let's say you want to be able to do 50 push-ups without stopping. You get on the floor and can barely squeeze out 10. How can you improve? Simple. You train those muscles (i.e. chest and triceps) in a pushup motion (specificity) every few days for about 3-6 months. As your body adapts to the stress of the force inputs from your push-ups, your muscles hypertrophy (cellular change) and your nerve system adapts to generate better force (connection) to those muscles for that movement. In six months you can drop down and bang out 50 push-ups! Hooray for you!

Now if I told you that you could just do a few push-ups a few times a month or less and magically end up being able to do 50, would you believe me? Or course not. So we need repeated force application through tissues (exercise) often enough to create a change in your body.

The exact same thing goes when it applies to changing the cellular structure and function of your tissues through chiropractic care!

Here's another example that I see all too often in my practice. Joe comes into the office with a history of recurrent back pain and stiffness spanning over 20 years. Examination findings reveal limits in spinal ranges of motion (joints are locked up) and his x-rays show degenerative changes to his lumbar discs and joints. Joe asks, "Dr. Pete, I hope you can fix me up with a good crack today. I've got a golf game this weekend AND my insurance only covers $300 for chiropractic so I can only come in a few times..."

I think to myself "Oh Joe...where do I begin with you?!"

Even if I gave Joe a spectacular chiropractic adjustment and he felt better, would that one adjustment create any long term change to the function of Joe's spine and the structure of his tissues? I hope you know the answer is NO WAY!

That is exactly why I wrote this book and exactly why you are reading it. I want you to understand the principles of how your body works and have realistic expectations and time frames to change how you function and feel so that the improvements are stable and long lasting.

This brings up another topic that I don't want to spend a great deal of time on: spending money on your health. In Canada we have been brought up to believe that health care should be "free". It's not free of course, it's paid for by our tax dollars. It would be wonderful if we had government or extended health coverage for all the care we want and need but this just isn't

realistic and I am sorry to inform you that you will probably be paying more and more out of pocket for health care as our current system hasn't operated particularly well, from a financial standpoint. So here's my sales job: YOU ARE VALUABLE. YOUR HEALTH IS PRICELESS. YOU CAN'T ENJOY ANYTHING IN YOUR LIFE IF YOU ARE IN PAIN OR NOT FUNCTIONING WELL. YOU SPEND $500-$1000 A MONTH ON YOUR CAR PAYMENT (YES YOU!!). ISN'T YOUR BODY THAT YOU LIVE IN MORE IMPORTANT THAN YOUR CAR THAT IN 5-10 YEARS WILL BE SCRAP METAL???
Okay that's enough. I will stop preaching :)

The second, scientifically rational way chiropractic adjustments may impact human function and well-being is via inputs to the nerve system.

As mentioned previously, our nerve system has bidirectional communication with the brain sending messages to the tissues via nerves (efference) and also receiving messages from nerve receptors in tissues (afference). In order for your brain to control your body it must receive proper signals or afference, especially from the joints in your spine. As the joints in your spine, pelvis and hips get locked up and lose their ability to move properly, your brain begins to be deprived of the afference needed to control your body accurately. Your brain, with a fuzzy or incomplete picture of your body, can no longer control your body properly, leading to poor function, injury and eventually pain. The consequence of this might be mild in a person with a very sedentary lifestyle, but for anyone who wishes to perform at a high level in sports or life, this is a big issue.

In the research world, spinal adjustments are referred to as spinal manipulative therapy or SMT for short. A number of studies have demonstrated that most SMT techniques provide a very significant amount of afference to the nerve system and brain that may act as a signal to normalize things like muscle tone (i.e. tight muscles relax and weak muscles get strong) [17]. This can be likened to what we all need to do with our smartphones and computers occasionally: turn them off and back on so they reset! It seems that many of the changes in function and feeling that are reported by patients after chiropractic adjustments are most likely due to the unique nerve system and brain changes from the significant afference that stems from a manual force input or adjustment [18]. This is really what makes a chiropractic adjustment stand out from other healthcare interventions; not that it's better but that it can do something that pretty much no other therapy or medication can for your nerve system.

So in some ways a chiropractic adjustment causing an influx of input to the brain and nerve system may help your musculoskeletal tissues reset so they can function normally. As your spine and joints have their normal function restored over time, the improved afference will literally allow your brain to control your body better, resulting in better coordination, strength, performance along with less chance of injury and pain.

A few small studies have also shown other relevant changes in overall brain function following chiropractic spinal adjustments. The study authors have concluded that there seems to be a shift towards sympathetic nerve system relaxation and neck muscle relaxation which may explain the feeling of ease, wellbeing, pain relief and relaxation often experienced after an adjustment [19, 20].

There is some recent research in press indicating improvements in Testosterone/Cortisol ratio and calf muscle blood oxygenation in patients with achilles tendinopathy after a single spinal adjustment to the thoracic spine (mid/upper back) [21]. The researcher indicated that these findings may indicate overall better functioning of the body physiology after an adjustment, although more studies need to be done to further clarify the precise potential benefits of these changes.

Chapter 8 - So you're thinking of seeing a Chiropractor?

If you are still reading this book you might be saying "okay Dr. Pete, maybe chiropractic care might be able to help me." Here's more on what conditions have good scientific validity indicating that chiropractic/spinal manipulative therapy can help you with:

Acute back and neck pain [22, 23]

Chronic low back pain - reducing pain and improving function [24]

Headaches and migraines [25, 26]

A review of research has also indicated evidence supporting chiropractic spinal manipulative therapy as beneficial for the following non- musculoskeletal conditions: asthma, cervicogenic vertigo, infantile colic, and possibly some subpopulations of hypertensives (patients with high blood pressure) [27].

Now for the most important question -
Will chiropractic be able to help YOU?

Well, you'll have to try it out so see. Of course there are no guarantees as with all forms of health care. In saying that though let's go back to the title of this book, "Function better, Feel Better". Research tells us that patients whose spinal function is changed after an adjustment experience improvements in pain, stiffness and disability [28]. Recent evidence has also shown that patients tend to respond better to chiropractic adjustments if they haven't developed joint degeneration and disc problems [29]. This is a really important reason why you shouldn't wait until your spine and joints are in big trouble before seeing a chiropractor! (Read more about this below)

In today's world, chiropractors are part of an individual's health care team. We don't replace medical or other care, but we do provide a unique element to your health by focusing primarily on the function of your spine and joints. Health care is changing, especially now with more and more medical care being done remotely (phone or video call) and patients receiving "hands on" care less and less. Chiropractic is the exception here. Because my patients see me more often than they do their medical doctor, and because I am so familiar with their health, I can often let patients know when they need to seek a medical opinion for new problems or things outside the scope of chiropractic. Many of my patients report that upon telling their medical doctor they are benefitting from seeing a chiropractor, their doctor is happy to know that they have found supportive care in a way they may not be able to provide through traditional means like medications.

Other reasons (maybe the most important) to see a chiropractor:

A chiropractor can examine your posture, spinal and other joint mobility and function and provide care, exercises and recommendations to help improve and maintain function. This could be really valuable to you and your family since being proactive and preventing loss of joint motion and degenerative changes will save you from unnecessary pain and suffering. As discussed in the previous chapter, chiropractic care and exercises can provide afference to your nerve system and brain that will help you perform better and avoid injury.

As one researcher has put it:

"It is hypothesized that because spinal manipulative therapy...encourages normal range of motion, routine manipulation of asymptomatic patients may retard the progression of joint degeneration, neuronal changes, changes in muscular strength, and recruitment patterns, which may result in improved function, decreased episodes of injuries, and improved sense of well-being [30]."

It's always tough for me to see a 50 or 60 year come into my office with years of uncorrected spinal and joint problems and hope for a miracle because they've tried everything else. We can still help people in this predicament but it's so much easier to maintain health than restore it when it is so far off track. It's also a lot more expensive! The reality is some people just don't think about keeping their health - usually because they are too busy caring for others (moms take note) or are too stressed and preoccupied with other aspects of their life like their career. Again, if this is you, don't beat yourself up. You're reading this at the right time, and chances are they'll be lots that can be done to improve how you function and feel no matter what you've been through or how old you are when you've decided to start taking care of yourself.

Chapter 9 - Your First Visit

Before your first visit to a chiropractor it would be useful if you could gather relevant information about yourself such as medications you are taking and any results of previous tests (x-rays, CT, MRI, ultrasound, blood work). You might also want to do a quick mental inventory of previous stresses - things like car accidents, falls, sports injuries, surgeries etc. so you have them top of mind when your chiropractic asks you about them. This is also a good time to think of the goals you'd like to achieve with your care. Things like reducing pain, improving mobility, getting back to working out, sleeping better etc.

A typical first chiropractic visit will involve completion of a health history followed by a consultation with the Doctor. During the consultation you'll have the opportunity to discuss your concerns and goals and the Doctor will ask a number of specific questions to learn about your problems and what you are looking for.

After the consultation, if the chiropractor thinks they can help you, you may consent to an examination of your spine, joints, soft tissues and more. In my office we routinely check new patients for postural deviations (i.e. forward head posture), and issues with balance and strength. Ranges of motion of spinal and other joints are usually assessed looking for pain, limitation and dysfunction. Relevant orthopedic and neurological testing may be done to help diagnose your problem. Spinal joint and other joint palpation is also usually done to assess for abnormal function along with associated assessment of soft-tissue structures (muscles, tendons, ligaments). In some cases, your

Doctor may recommend taking spinal or joint x-rays to check for the presence of abnormal curves or pathologies such as disc and joint degeneration. X-rays can be very useful as they help establish a timeline of just how long your joints may have been dysfunctional before your symptoms started. This helps with accurate care planning so that the Doctor can come up with realistic expectations for how long you may need care for improvements to occur.

After your exam is completed, your Doctor is required to present the findings from your tests so that they help you understand where and how your body may not be functioning normally and what things can be done to help improve how you are functioning and feeling. You will be given a diagnosis related to your spine, joints and nerve system and a plan of care will be presented in order to correct your functional problems over time. Your Doctor will also be required to take you through the process of informed consent, which includes reviewing the potential benefits and risks of the proposed treatment, other alternatives you may explore as well as any possible consequences of not receiving the proposed care. I also inform my patients that informed consent is an ongoing process, so if at any point they would like to alter or stop their care they may do so. This is the point where I ask all my patients: "Does what we've gone over make sense to you? Do you feel that you'd like to start the proposed care plan with me?" If I don't get a "YES" here we stop and don't proceed. I know from my many years working with human beings that an individual must feel comfortable not only with the proposed treatment but also with the fact that I will be delivering it. There are plenty of possible reasons why care may not be right for an individual at a particular time including difficulties with their schedule, their level of priority to correct their problems, their willingness to pay out of pocket to improve their health and more. I will discuss all these issues and if we can come to an agreement we'll start care, but if not we'll hold off. And that's perfectly fine.

Sometimes a patient will ask if they can try a few adjustments and see how they feel. I've done this with a number of individuals and for some reason, I'm not exactly sure why, the results are never satisfactory for the patient or me. Can you think of why this might be the case? I'm not entirely sure but I think it's kind of akin to someone saying they are going to do a few workouts before they decide if they want to commit to a fitness plan. They are kind of on the fence and their mind is split about what they should do rather than 100% committed. Again I'll state that it's completely fine that a patient be unsure what to do, but in those cases I've found it's best to hold off on care until they make a clear decision one way or the other. Bottom line is I like working with patients who are excited and motivated to come to the office and receive care!

I should mention that the care that I and most chiropractors provide to our patients goes beyond adjusting. When they are ready, I give my patients specific mobility exercises to help improve their joint health and nerve system function. Many of my patients also are looking for help with things like stress management so I often recommend and give instruction on things such as deep breathing and meditation.

At this point I want to give you the most valuable piece of advice regarding your chiropractic care from my 15+ years of working with patients: CONSISTENCY MATTERS.

As discussed previously our body has the ability to remodel its tissues, and in fact is continually remodeling (cells dying and being replaced by new ones) with the pattern for remodeling based on what you do or don't do over time. I've seen many patients have fantastic improvements in their pain, health and mobility over months of consistent care and lifestyle changes. I've also seen one too many patients who didn't follow their care plan (they came sporadically for visits) and didn't follow their lifestyle recommendations and…they end up with the same bad feeling, bad functioning body. Don't let this be you! You've already heard me preach about the value of caring for your health so I don't want to beat you over the head with this message any more :) Remember that in the big scheme of things it usually only takes a few visits to the office a week, along with a few minutes a day of some targeted exercises and meditation to get some great results over time. That's what I want for you!

During an individual's chiropractic care periodic re-exams are done to assess progress, determine any changes that need to be made with the care plan along with discussion of future goals. Again please remember that the time it takes for you to experience improvements is usually related to how long your body has been functioning improperly (not necessarily how long you've had your symptoms).

And the great news is that once your spine, joints and nerve system begins to function better, the frequency of your visits can be reduced, especially when you are taking the time to do your home exercises. So after your initial corrective care is completed properly you can maintain your improvements with a lot less frequent visits which means less time and money!

Chapter 10 - The Safety of Chiropractic Care

Maybe you've never heard much about chiropractic care and this book is your first exposure to it...or

Maybe you've heard horror stories. "Chiropractic adjustments can hurt, break your bones, cause a stroke, make you weak, make you worse, aren't safe for kids, make you have to go forever..."

Lots of emotion here, often from well-meaning people.

But, let's go to the evidence.

What does the scientific literature say are the risks associated with spinal manipulation?

A review of over 50 studies published in 2018 concluded that spinal manipulation for low back pain is safe, with occasional side effects being "mild, including temporary treatment-related soreness, tiredness, or worsening of existing complaints [24]."

This is pretty much what I see in practice - yes you can have some mild short term soreness especially when starting care. For reasons not fully understood some patients experience significant improvement the day after their adjustment. I've wondered if this has to do with the fact that the brain and nerve system make alterations to function when the body and mind rest during sleep.

The old school chiropractors would always make sure their patients rested, in some cases for hours after an adjustment.

When I am dealing with patients who are in a lot of pain or who are dealing with a high amount of stress I ask them to go home after their visit, put their feet up, take a nap, have a good meal and just RELAX. Easy for me to say, hard for some to follow through with, but this seems to often produce improvement!

What about cracking joints? Isn't that bad for you and can cause arthritis? In short, the evidence says no. A recent study showed that the "cracking" that is heard and felt when a joint is moved (by a chiropractor or by yourself) is due to the sudden separation of joint surfaces [31], and repeatedly doing so does not seem to cause osteoarthritis [32].

What about kids?

A literature review of chiropractic care in children found that adverse events were rare with no deaths reported in the literature [33].

Can a chiropractic adjustment cause a stroke? What about those few stories of people who allegedly went to a chiropractor and they sometime later had a stroke?

To understand this question we have to go to the basic scientific principle that correlation does not equal causation. In other words when two things occur closely in time that doesn't always mean that the prior caused the latter. I remember some Italian relatives telling me that it was an absolute rule that older individuals should never get up at night and drink water. Why? Because they had heard stories of people who did this and didn't wake up the next morning because they'd died of a heart attack. Their conclusion: drinking water at night can cause death by heart attack. Of course this is ridiculous and not supported at all by any science. But that didn't stop this myth from being propagated through generations of Italians. What probably happened in these cases were people feeling unwell and thirsty in the early stages of a heart attack, and of course what happened first (the drinking of water) didn't CAUSE the heart attack.

This story is very similar to the "I heard of somebody who went and had their neck manipulated and then had a stroke". I've even heard this come out of the mouths of some well-intentioned but very poorly (scientifically) informed doctors and neurologists.

An excellent review study was done by investigators from the Department of Neurosurgery at Penn State University who concluded: "There is no convincing evidence to support a causal link between chiropractic manipulation and cervical artery dissection (stroke). Belief in a causal link may have significant negative consequences such as numerous episodes of litigation [34]."

What may have happened in these stories mentioned above is that a person went to a chiropractor with neck pain and headache (possible early signs of stroke). Some time after their adjustment their stroke worsened and caused symptoms. So the person (or possibly doctor attending to them) mistakenly attributed the stroke to the adjustment that happened hours or days (even months) before. Just like our drinking water at night heart attack story.

Not only does the research not support a causal link between neck manipulation and stroke, there also exists evidence that shows it's probably not even possible. This is from research done at the University of Calgary that demonstrated that the forces that go through the arteries of the neck during an adjustment are essentially the same as when we do everyday neck movements like turning our head or looking up and down [35]. The forces during a neck adjustment are also many times below the force levels required to cause artery damage seen in a stroke [35]. The last thing I want is any of my patients having fear of something that research has essentially proved doesn't exist!

One thing I'd like to mention here is that human nature seems to dictate that we are more afraid of activities that we don't usually engage in compared to those that we do, that are actually more dangerous. The risk of death from commercial flying is approximately 1 in 9,821, while the risk of death of dying in a car accident is 1 in 114 [36]. Are you or any of your friends afraid to get in your car? Very unlikely! It's much more likely that you or one of your friends are afraid of flying although it is many times safer!

Of course, there are also risks to not taking care of your spine and joints. Allowing your spine, joints and nerve system to deteriorate, leading to pain and reduced mobility can have serious implications for your health, especially in the area of aging. If you can't exercise, move easily, drive a car, care for yourself or require medications for pain and symptom relief (which have side effects) then those are all very real risks to your health.

One really important area being looked at currently is chiropractic with respect to fall risk in the elderly which is a huge problem in this age group. Preliminary evidence has indicated that chiropractic may play a role in fall prevention in elderly persons with neck pain and dizziness [37].

One last thing on safety. Chiropractors pay the lowest malpractice insurance premiums compared to any other type of Doctor [38]. Bet you can guess why - we get sued the least because our care is generally very safe!

Now, you might be thinking “that’s fine Dr. Pete you have lots of research to back up your points, but what has happened in your practice?”

I’ll give you an honest answer. Since opening my doors in late 2005 I have delivered an estimated 300,000 adjustments. No strokes. I have had a number of patients have soreness after an adjustment especially if they were in rough shape when starting care but this isn’t the norm. Soreness after care for new patients is kind of akin to how a person would have soreness when starting a new activity or exercise routine - it tends to be mild and to subside as the tissues get used to the new movement. I have had two instances out of my thousands of patient interactions where I know my adjustment sprained a rib, both cases in elderly women and in both cases these patients healed without incident. I make every effort to perform care in a way that is safe for my patients. I never force a patient to receive care or a particular style of adjustment if they are not comfortable with it. I’m certainly not perfect but I do pride myself on delivering safe effective care and continuing to refine my craft. And that’s the truth!

Chapter 11 - Case Studies

I've had so many patients get great results with their chiropractic care of the years there are way too many to share. But here are a select few that might give you an idea of what may be possible for you:

Case Study - Chronic Low Back Pain

A 50 year old male had been suffering with chronic low back pain and sciatica with episodes that had been getting progressively worse, His job required him to sit at a desk and work on a computer all day which seemed to aggravate his condition. Most concerning to this individual was that he had not been able to golf the previous year before coming to my office. This individual was examined and x-rays revealed early degenerative disc and joint problems in his lower back (lumbar) vertebrae at L4/5 and L5/S1. He began a course of chiropractic care, initially coming three times per week for full spine adjustments. As his function improved his care was reduced to once weekly and then biweekly visits. He was also given specific mobility exercises that he did at home daily. The patient's low back pain and sciatica improved to where after six months of care he was completely symptom free. The patient was very happy with his results as he was able to resume playing golf several times per week with no pain or spinal issues!

Case Study - Headaches

A 35 year old female had been suffering from neck pain, 3x weekly headaches and fatigue/poor sleep for 10+ years. Her headaches and never feeling rested were making it difficult for her to do her job which required long hours of intense work as well as caring for her family. Her exam revealed restrictions in cervical (neck) range of motion along with segmental tender spinal restrictions in her upper back and upper neck. She began a course of chiropractic adjustments to her affected areas and experienced incremental improvements over a three month period to where her headaches and neck pain had mostly resolved except for very stressful days of work. She also began sleeping better and indicated that her energy levels were the best they'd been in years. She is benefitting from improved health and energy from her chiropractic care as are her employer and family!

Case Study - Workout performance

A 40 year old male came to the office for an evaluation because he'd heard that he should have his spine checked by a chiropractor. He did not have any significant pain or issues but had a history of a whiplash injury from a car accident as well as recent onset of high intensity crossfit style exercise after being sedentary for a number of years. Examination of his spine and joints revealed tender, restricted spinal segments in his mid-back and lower neck, as well as restricted active and passive ranges of hip motion on both sides. Chiropractic care was started to improve spinal and hip joint function. The patient noticed that he could run faster/easier during his workouts after starting care and also felt that his weight lifting performance was improved and he was less likely to feel neck and back tightness after training.

To see more real life examples of how chiropractic care has benefitted people just like you please check out my YouTube videos here: https://www.youtube.com/drpeterangerilli

Chapter 12 - What's next for you?

Thanks for sticking with me through this book. I want to mention a few general health recommendations that I think all of us should be doing daily regardless of whether or not you're seeing a chiropractor.

1. Move your joints daily.

Remember our joints are kept healthy by regular movement. Start with the basics like a short walk every day. Things like weight training, yoga, crossfit, recreational sports and even house and yard work can count towards this. The best option is to work towards specifically putting each of your joints from your toes to your neck through their full ranges of motion every day. I am working on an instructional video you can follow to learn these movements so please check back to my YouTube page in the future where this content will be available.

2. Meditate daily

I'm not trying to turn you into a monk here but we know that meditation with deep slow breathing has benefits to the body and mind. Deep breathing also moves our spine and ribcage so it is a useful way to get mobility into these joints. I have to tell you that I ask most of my patients to do deep breathing meditation 10-15 minutes and day and most...don't! That is until they eventually try and get hooked like I did. Here's how I do it: I go into a quiet room where I am free of distractions (background noise is okay). I set my iPhone timer for 15 minutes. I close my eyes and focus my mind on breathing, aiming for six second inhalations and six second exhalations. Simple. Well, simple in theory, but not easy, but definitely worth it. This practice can help relieve muscle tension, pain and bring wellbeing, all natural and without side effects. Try it!

3. Take rest breaks

This is another one that I tell most people to do, and most don't. I don't know if it's that people are afraid of being accused of being lazy if they lie down during the day (I don't have that problem apparently). If possible, lie down to get gravity off your spine and joints sometime during your day. If you have the time and feel like it you can also take a short nap to refresh and recharge. I do this every day and notice that it helps me stay mentally alert and energized well into the evening. I know this isn't of course feasible for everybody depending on work and family schedules. But even if you are out all day consider putting your feet up for a few minutes when you get home and allowing your body and mind to calm. For many, dinner is the biggest meal of the day and your body will be in a much better state to digest your food when you are relaxed rather than tense.

4. Take care of yourself and take responsibility for your health

Guess who is responsible for their heath? YOU! I can hear you now "but Dr. Pete I'm so busy taking care of my kids/grandkids/elderly parents/working etc. etc. that I simply can't take the time or energy to take care of my health'. To this I say: You can take a few minutes a day to take care of your health now, OR you can wait until you get a sickness or problem and then spend all day on the couch, in bed, or waiting in hospitals or Doctors' offices, unable to take care of the people you care about. Besides, as we already established earlier in this book, you will be a much better parent, grandparent, employee, business owner, athlete etc. when you are functioning and feeling well!

And finally if you feel inspired to...

Get to a chiropractor, and have your spine, joints and nerve system examined.

If you have questions, get them answered, email me drpeterangerilli@gmail.com

If you made it this far through my book I want to reward you! Mention code ALIGNMENT and you can come to my office and get your initial comprehensive spine, joint and nerve system examination, valued at $85, for free!
To schedule this visit please call my office at 905-634-9494.

My office is located at 2012 Victoria Avenue in Burlington, Ontario. We are a short drive from many areas in the Greater Toronto Area and see patients from Hamilton, Oakville, Mississauga, Niagara region and more.

Of course you don't have to see me, as there are many great chiropractors all across Canada and the U.S. who can help you when you are ready.

Here are some resources that you may find helpful:

My website: http://clearviewchiropractic.ca

My YouTube channel with patient videos and more:
https://www.youtube.com/drpeterangerilli

Office Facebook Page:
https://www.facebook.com/ClearviewChiropractic/

Dr. Pete's Instagram:
https://www.instagram.com/drpeteangerilli/?hl=en

And finally...If you are functioning and feeling better because of something you read in this book, send me an email or message letting me know! I'd love to hear from you!

Yours in Health,

Dr. Pete

References

[1] College of Chiropractors of Ontario. Scope of Practice and Authorized Acts. https://www.cco.on.ca/members-of-the-public/scope-of-practice-and-authorized-acts/. Published 2018. Accessed July 12, 2020.

[2] Setton LA, Elliott DM, Mow VC. Altered mechanics of cartilage with osteoarthritis: human osteoarthritis and an experimental model of joint degeneration. *Osteoarthritis and Cartilage*. 1999;7(1):2-14. doi:10.1053/joca.1998.0170

[3] Guilak F. Biomechanical factors in osteoarthritis. *Best Pract Res Clin Rheumatol*. 2011;25(6):815-823. doi:10.1016/j.berh.2011.11.013

[4] Wulsin L, Herman J, Thayer JF. Stress, autonomic imbalance, and the prediction of metabolic risk: A model and a proposal for research. Neuroscience and biobehavioral reviews. https://www.ncbi.nlm.nih.gov/pubmed/29277456. Published March 2018. Accessed July 12, 2020.

[5] Sapolsky RM. Why Zebras Don't Get Ulcers: an Updated Guide to Stress, Stress-Related Diseases, and Coping. New York: Owl; 2004.

[6] Pettman E. A History of Manipulative Therapy. Journal of Manual & Manipulative Therapy. 2007;15(3):165-174. doi:10.1179/106698107790819873

[7] Maynard JE. Healing Hands: The Story of the Palmer Family - Discoverers and Developers of Chiropractic. 4th ed. Long Island, NY: Jonorm Publishers; 1992.

[8] Budgell, B. The Harvey Lilard Story. [Video]. YouTube. https://www.youtube.com/watch?v=sa99fOT1Oxk. Published September 10, 2012. Accessed July 14, 2020.

[9] Palmer BJ. Chiropractic Clinical Controlled Research. Davenport, IA: Palmer College of Chiropractic; 1951.

[10] Quigley H. Clear View Sanitarium, Part 5. Dynamic Chiropractic - chiropractic, news, articles, research & information for chiropractors. https://www.dynamicchiropractic.com/mpacms/dc/article.php?id=45215. Published April 11, 1990. Accessed July 12, 2020.

[11] Kent, Christopher. (2013). Chiropractic and Mental Health: A Brief Overview. J. Philosophy, Principles & Practice of Chiropractic. 2013. 1.

[12] King HH, Patterson MM, Jänig Wilfrid, Triano JJ. Survey of mechanotransduction disorders. In: The Science and Clinical Application of Manual Therapy. Edinburgh: Churchill Livingstone; 2011:93-107.

[13] Paluch EK, Nelson CM, Biais N, et al. Mechanotransduction: use the force(s). BMC Biology. 2015;13(1). doi:10.1186/s12915-015-0150-4

[14] Henderson CN, Cramer GD, Zhang Q, Devocht JW, Fournier JT. Introducing the External Link Model for Studying Spine Fixation and Misalignment. Journal of Manipulative and Physiological Therapeutics. 2007;30(3):239-245. doi:10.1016/j.jmpt.2007.01.006

[15] Henderson CN, Cramer GD, Zhang Q, Devocht JW, Fournier JT. Introducing the External Link Model for Studying Spine Fixation and Misalignment: Part 2, Biomechanical Features. Journal of Manipulative and Physiological Therapeutics. 2007;30(4):279-294. doi:10.1016/j.jmpt.2007.03.002

[16] Dong S, Xie G, Zhang Y, Shen P, Huangfu X, Zhao J. Ligamentization of Autogenous Hamstring Grafts After Anterior Cruciate Ligament Reconstruction. The American Journal of Sports Medicine. 2015;43(8):1908-1917. doi:10.1177/0363546515584039

[17] Smith, D. (Host). Chiropractic neurophysiology with Dr. Bernadette Murphy. Chiropractic Science. 2015 Jan 16. Retrieved from https://chiropracticscience.com/

Ogura T, Tashiro M, Masud M, et al. Cerebral metabolic changes in men after chiropractic spinal manipulation for neck pain. Altern Ther Health Med. 2011;17(6):12-17.

[18] Gyer G, Michael J, Inklebarger J, Tedla JS. Spinal manipulation therapy: Is it all about the brain? A current review of the neurophysiological effects of manipulation. Journal of Integrative Medicine. 2019;17(5):328-337. doi:10.1016/j.joim.2019.05.004

[19] Ogura, Takeshi & Tashiro, Manabu & Masud, Mehedi & Watanuki, Shoichi & Shibuya, Katsuhiko & Yamaguchi, Keiichiro & Itoh, Masatoshi & Fukuda, Hiroshi & Yanai, Kazuhiko. (2011). Cerebral metabolic changes in men after chiropractic spinal manipulation for neck pain. Alternative therapies in health and medicine. 17. 12-7.

[20] Inami A, Ogura T, Watanuki S, et al. Glucose Metabolic Changes in the Brain and Muscles of Patients with Nonspecific Neck Pain Treated by Spinal Manipulation Therapy: A [18F]FDG PET Study. Evid Based Complement Alternat Med. 2017;2017:4345703. doi:10.1155/2017/4345703

[21] Angerilli, P. How spinal adjusting may affect the neuroendocrine system - An interview with researcher Dr. Kesava Sampath [Video]. YouTube. https://www.youtube.com/watch?v=TjVv2dxMYWE&t=626s. Published September 30, 2019. Accesed July 12, 2020.

[22] Qaseem A, Wilt TJ, Mclean RM, Forciea MA. Noninvasive Treatments for Acute, Subacute, and Chronic Low Back Pain: A Clinical Practice Guideline From the American College of Physicians. Annals of Internal Medicine. 2017;166(7):514. doi:10.7326/m16-2367

[23] Wong JJ, Shearer HM, Mior S, et al. Are manual therapies, passive physical modalities, or acupuncture effective for the management of patients with whiplash-associated disorders or neck pain and associated disorders? An update of the Bone and Joint Decade Task Force on Neck Pain and Its Associated

Disorders by the OPTIMa collaboration. The Spine Journal. 2016;16(12):1598-1630. doi:10.1016/j.spinee.2015.08.024

[24] Coulter ID, Crawford C, Hurwitz EL, et al. Manipulation and mobilization for treating chronic low back pain: a systematic review and meta-analysis. The Spine Journal. 2018;18(5):866-879. doi:10.1016/j.spinee.2018.01.013

[25] Mesa-Jiménez JA, Lozano-López C, Angulo-Díaz-Parreño S, Rodríguez-Fernández ÁL, De-La-Hoz-Aizpurua JL, Fernández-De-Las-Peñas C. Multimodal manual therapy vs. pharmacological care for management of tension type headache: A meta-analysis of randomized trials. Cephalalgia. 2015;35(14):1323-1332. doi:10.1177/0333102415576226

[26] Chaibi A, Tuchin PJ, Russell MB. Manual therapies for migraine: a systematic review. The Journal of Headache and Pain. 2011;12(2):127-133. doi:10.1007/s10194-011-0296-6

[27] Hawk C, Khorsan R, Lisi AJ, Ferrance RJ, Evans MW. Chiropractic Care for Nonmusculoskeletal Conditions: A Systematic Review with Implications for Whole Systems Research. The Journal of Alternative and Complementary Medicine. 2007;13(5):491-512. doi:10.1089/acm.2007.7088

[28] Wong AY, Parent EC, Dhillon SS, Prasad N, Kawchuk GN. Do participants with low back pain who respond to spinal manipulative therapy differ biomechanically from nonresponders, untreated controls or asymptomatic controls?. Spine (Phila Pa 1976). 2015;40(17):1329-1337. doi:10.1097/BRS.0000000000000981

[29] Wong AYL, Parent EC, Dhillon SS, Prasad N, Samartzis D, Kawchuk GN. Differential patient responses to spinal manipulative therapy and their relation to spinal degeneration and post-treatment changes in disc diffusion. Eur Spine J. 2019;28(2):259-269. doi:10.1007/s00586-018-5851-2

[30] Taylor DN. A theoretical basis for maintenance spinal manipulative therapy for the chiropractic profession. Journal of Chiropractic Humanities. 2011;18(1):74-85. doi:10.1016/j.echu.2011.07.001

[31] Kawchuk GN, Fryer J, Jaremko JL, Zeng H, Rowe L, Thompson R (2015) Real-Time Visualization of Joint Cavitation. PLoS ONE 10(4): e0119470. https://doi.org/10.1371/journal.pone.0119470

[32] Deweber K, Olszewski M, Ortolano R. Knuckle Cracking and Hand Osteoarthritis. The Journal of the American Board of Family Medicine. 2011;24(2):169-174. doi:10.3122/jabfm.2011.02.100156

[33] Todd AJ, Carroll MT, Robinson A, Mitchell EK. Adverse Events Due to Chiropractic and Other Manual Therapies for Infants and Children: A Review of the Literature. Journal of Manipulative and Physiological Therapeutics. 2015;38(9):699-712. doi:10.1016/j.jmpt.2014.09.008

[34] Church EW, Sieg EP, Zalatimo O, Hussain NS, Glantz M, Harbaugh RE. Systematic Review and Meta-analysis of Chiropractic Care and Cervical Artery Dissection: No Evidence for Causation. Cureus. 2016;8(2):e498. Published 2016 Feb 16. doi:10.7759/cureus.498

[35] Symons BP, Leonard T, Herzog W. Internal forces sustained by the vertebral artery during spinal manipulative therapy. J Manipulative Physiol Ther. 2002;25(8):504-510. doi:10.1067/mmt.2002.127076

[36] Jenkins A. Which Is Safer: Airplanes or Cars? Fortune. https://fortune.com/2017/07/20/are-airplanes-safer-than-cars/. Published January 15, 2020. Accessed July 12, 2020.

[37] Kendall JC, Hartvigsen J, French SD, Azari MF. Is there a role for neck manipulation in elderly falls prevention? - An overview. J Can Chiropr Assoc. 2015;59(1):53-63.

[38] Heid M. Are Chiropractors Legitimate? Time. https://time.com/4282617/chiropractor-lower-back-pain/. Published December 6, 2019. Accessed July 12, 2020.